SCHOLASTIC

Grades 4–6

Leveled Nonfiction Passages
for Building
Comprehension

CAROL GHIGLIERI

New York • Toronto • London • Auckland • Sydney
Mexico City • New Delhi • Hong Kong • Buenos Aires

Teaching *Resources*

Cover design by Jason Robinson
Interior illustrations by Mike Moran
Interior design by Kelli Thompson

ISBN: 978-0-545-22756-8

Contents

Introduction

Welcome to *Leveled Nonfiction Passages for Building Comprehension*, a collection of 36 high-interest passages and accompanying comprehension questions. This assortment of nonfiction passages, written at three different reading levels—low, medium, and high—covers a range of intriguing topics that will appeal to kids in grades 4 to 6 and motivate all your readers.

Why Nonfiction?

It's no secret that as students move up in grade level they encounter more nonfiction material—and that this material becomes increasingly complex in content, style, and structure. In addition, nonfiction accounts for about half of the passages they will find on standardized tests. So it's crucial that students become capable readers of nonfiction.

Nonfiction poses a different set of challenges than fiction does. Whereas fiction tells a story, nonfiction presents facts, ideas, and information. Students need to learn how to comprehend that information in order to succeed in school and in the real world.

Leveled Passages for Differentiation

This book provides 12 passages, each written at three readability levels ranging from 2.5 to 8, according to the Flesch-Kincaid readability formula. In addition to the readability score, other factors that determine the difficulty of the passages include:

- Vocabulary
- Sentence structure
- Use of figurative language/idioms
- Complexity of ideas

Throughout the book, the three levels are signaled by three different icons:

Low: ◆
Medium: ●
High: ⬟

Along with the passages themselves, the comprehension questions accompanying each passage increase in their level of challenge as well. The passages are arranged in the book by readability score, so that more difficult passages occur later.

Note: In calculating the low readability score of 4.0 for "What's the Point of Acupuncture?" (page 60) I omitted the word "acupuncture," which is necessary for understanding the text, but challenging for most students. You might want to introduce the word to students before they read.

Comprehension Questions

The questions that follow each passage will help you assess students' understanding of the material and give them practice answering test questions. The questions target a range of comprehension skills that frequently appear on standardized tests, including making inferences, finding the main idea, and vocabulary knowledge.

Ways to Use the Passages

The passages are designed to be used flexibly, allowing you to differentiate instruction for the varied learners in your classroom. Use the passages to:

- Practice reading comprehension
- Explore nonfiction
- Prepare for standardized tests
- Motivate struggling readers

Written about a variety of topics that appeal to fourth- to sixth-graders, these passages can help you reach all the readers in your classroom. Students will enjoy the material and build comprehension skills at the same time!

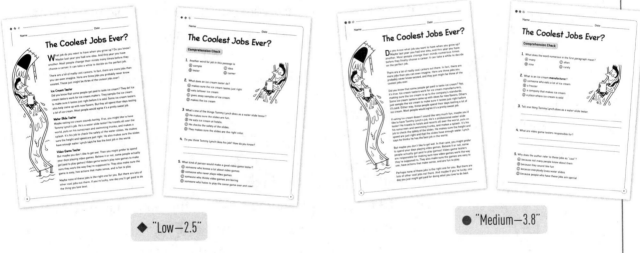

◆ "Low—2.5"

● "Medium—3.8"

Each passage set includes a short, nonfiction article written at a low, medium, and high level and a page of comprehension questions for each level.

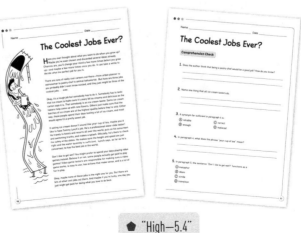

⬟ "High—5.4"

The Coolest Jobs Ever?

What job do you want to have when you grow up? Do you know? Maybe last year you had one idea. And this year you have another. Most people change their minds many times before they choose a career. It can take a while to decide on the perfect job.

There are a lot of really cool careers. In fact, there are more jobs than you can even imagine. Here are three jobs you probably never know existed. These just might be three of the coolest jobs ever!

Ice Cream Taster

Did you know that some people get paid to taste ice cream? They do! Ice cream tasters work for ice cream makers. They sample the ice cream to make sure it tastes just right before it is sold. Some ice cream tasters also help come up with new flavors. But they all spend their days tasting a lot of ice cream. Most people would agree it's a pretty sweet job.

Water Slide Tester

Maybe eating ice cream sounds boring. If so, you might like to have Tommy Lynch's job. He's a water slide tester! He travels all over the world, puts on his sunscreen and swimming trunks, and makes a splash. It's his job to check the safety of the water slides. He makes sure the height and speed are just right. He also makes sure the slides have enough water. Lynch says he has the best job in the world.

Video Game Tester

But maybe you don't like to get wet. Then you might prefer to spend your days playing video games. Believe it or not, some people actually get paid to play games! Video game testers play new games to make sure they work the way they're supposed to. They also make sure the game is easy, has actions that make sense, and is fun to play.

Maybe none of these jobs is the right one for you. But there are lots of other cool jobs out there. If you're lucky, one day you'll get paid to do the thing you love best.

The Coolest Jobs Ever?

Comprehension Check

1. Another word for *job* in this passage is
   - (A) sample
   - (B) tester
   - (C) idea
   - (D) career

2. What does an ice cream taster do?
   - (A) makes sure the ice cream tastes just right
   - (B) eats leftover ice cream
   - (C) gives away samples of ice cream
   - (D) makes the ice cream

3 What's one of the things Tommy Lynch does as a water slide tester?
   - (A) He makes sure the slides are fun.
   - (B) He eats ice cream at hotels.
   - (C) He checks the safety of the slides.
   - (D) They makes sure the slides are the right color.

4. Do you think Tommy Lynch likes his job? How do you know?

   _____

   _____

5. What kind of person would make a good video game tester?
   - (A) someone who knows a lot about video games
   - (B) someone who never plays video games
   - (C) someone who thinks video games are boring
   - (D) someone who hates to play the same game over and over

The Coolest Jobs Ever?

Do you know what job you want to have when you grow up? Maybe last year you had one idea, and this year you have another. Most people change their minds numerous times before they finally choose a career. It can take a while to decide on the perfect job.

There are a lot of really cool careers out there. In fact, there are more jobs than you can even imagine. Here are three jobs you probably never know existed, and they just might be three of the coolest jobs ever.

Did you know that some people get paid to taste ice cream? Yep, it's true. Ice cream tasters work for ice cream manufacturers, making sure the ice cream is up to the company's standards. Some ice cream tasters come up with ideas for new flavors. Others just sample the ice cream to make sure it tastes just right before it's sold. Either way, these people spend their days tasting a lot of ice cream. Most people would agree it's a pretty sweet job.

If eating ice cream doesn't sound like very much fun, maybe you'd like to have Tommy Lynch's job. He's a professional water slide tester! He travels to hotels and resorts all over the world, puts on his sunscreen and swimming trunks, and makes a splash. It's his job to check the safety of the slides. He makes sure the height and speed are just right and that the slides have enough water. Lynch says he thinks he has the best job in the world.

But maybe you don't like to get wet. In that case, you might prefer to spend your days playing video games. Believe it or not, some people actually get paid to play games! Video game testers are responsible for making sure new video games work the way they're supposed to. They also make sure the games are easy to use, have actions that make sense, and are fun to play.

Perhaps none of these jobs is the right one for you. But there are lots of other cool jobs out there. And maybe if you're lucky, one day you just might get paid for doing what you love to do best.

The Coolest Jobs Ever?

Comprehension Check

1. What does the word *numerous* in the first paragraph mean?

Ⓐ many   Ⓒ often

Ⓑ nine   Ⓓ rarely

2. What is an ice cream **manufacturer**?

Ⓐ someone who eats a lot of ice cream

Ⓑ a freezer

Ⓒ a company that makes ice cream

Ⓓ a place where ice cream is sold

3. Tell one thing Tommy Lynch does as a water slide tester.

_____

_____

4. What are video game testers responsible for?

_____

_____

5. Why does the author refer to these jobs as "cool"?

Ⓐ because not many people know about them

Ⓑ because they sound like fun

Ⓒ because everybody loves water slides

Ⓓ because people who have these jobs are special

The Coolest Jobs Ever?

Have you ever thought about what you want to do when you grow up? Maybe you've even chosen and discarded several ideas already. Chances are, you'll change your mind a few more times before you grow up—and maybe a few more times once you do. It can take a while to decide what the perfect job for you is.

There are tons of really cool careers out there—from urban planner to astronomer to pastry chef to animal behaviorist. But here are three jobs you probably didn't even know existed, and they just might be three of the coolest jobs . . . ever.

Okay, it's a tough job but somebody has to do it. Somebody has to taste that ice cream to make sure it's every bit as creamy and delicious as the carton says it is. That somebody is an ice cream taster. Some ice cream tasters help come up with new flavors. Others just make sure that the batches of ice cream are of the highest quality before they're sold. Either way, these people spend their days tasting a lot of ice cream, and most would agree it's a pretty sweet job.

If eating ice cream doesn't sound like your cup of tea, maybe you'd like to have Tommy Lynch's job. He's a professional water slide tester! He travels to hotels and resorts all over the world, puts on his sunscreen and swimming trunks, and makes a splash. Officially, he's there to check the safety of the slides. He makes sure the height and speed are just right and the water quantity is sufficient. Lynch says, as far as he's concerned, he has the best job in the world.

Don't like to get wet? You might prefer to spend your days playing video games instead. Believe it or not, some people actually get paid to play games! Video game testers are responsible for making sure a video game works, is easy to use, has actions that make sense, and is a lot of fun to play.

Okay, maybe none of these jobs is the right one for you. But there are lots of other cool jobs out there. And maybe if you're lucky, one day you just might get paid for doing what you love to do best.

The Coolest Jobs Ever?

Comprehension Check

1. Does the author think that being a pastry chef would be a good job? How do you know?

_____

_____

2. Name one thing that all ice cream tasters do.

_____

_____

3. A synonym for *sufficient* in paragraph 4 is:

  Ⓐ reliable   Ⓒ correct

  Ⓑ enough   Ⓓ replaced

4. In paragraph 4, what does the phrase "your cup of tea" mean?

_____

_____

5. In paragraph 5, the sentence "Don't like to get wet?" functions as a

  Ⓐ metaphor

  Ⓑ idiom

  Ⓒ simile

  Ⓓ transition

Busy Bees

Have you ever been stung by a bee? If you have, you might think bees are a big pain. But think again! Bees are some of nature's hardest workers. And without them, you might have a lot less to eat.

If you like the taste of honey, you can thank those buzzing bees. Each spring and summer, bees fly around to lots of flowers. They're hunting for nectar. Nectar is a sweet liquid inside of flowers. The bees suck the nectar from the flowers. They keep it in their stomachs until they get home.

The bees' home is called a hive. When bees get back to the hive, they empty the nectar from their stomachs. Then they let it sit for about five days. During this time, it gets very thick and turns into honey. At that point, it's ready for the bees to eat. Humans can eat it, too!

Bees also collect pollen to eat. They gather pollen from flowers and carry it home in sacks on their legs. But they also spread some of the pollen to other flowers. This is how the plants are pollinated, allowing them to bear fruit. Apples, pears, peaches, and almonds, are just some of the tasty foods that bees help make possible.

And what about those painful bee stings? A bee sting hurts the bee a lot more than it hurts you. Once a bee stings someone, it dies. Bees only sting people when they're afraid. If you don't bug them, they won't bug you. In truth, bees are amazing insects. They're not a pain at all!

Busy Bees

Comprehension Check

1. What is the name of a bee's home?
   - Ⓐ honey
   - Ⓒ pollen
   - Ⓑ hive
   - Ⓓ nectar

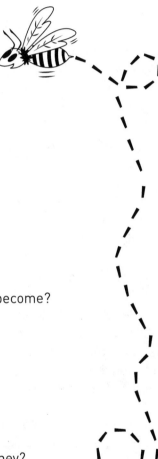

2. Where do bees store the pollen they collect?
   - Ⓐ in their stomachs
   - Ⓑ in the flowers
   - Ⓒ in sacks on their legs
   - Ⓓ in sacks on their wings

3. After bees gather nectar from the flowers, what does it become?
   - Ⓐ pollen
   - Ⓑ honey
   - Ⓒ peaches
   - Ⓓ wax

4. How many days does it take for the nectar to become honey?

   _____

5. Why does the author say that bees are amazing insects?
   - Ⓐ because when they sting someone they die
   - Ⓑ because they play a part in bringing us lots of food
   - Ⓒ because bees like honey, just like we do
   - Ⓓ because bees eat pollen

Busy Bees

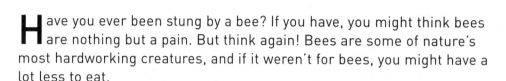

Have you ever been stung by a bee? If you have, you might think bees are nothing but a pain. But think again! Bees are some of nature's most hardworking creatures, and if it weren't for bees, you might have a lot less to eat.

That honey on your toast? You have bees to thank for it. During the spring and summer, bees visit flower after flower, gathering nectar from deep inside the blossoms. They suck the sweet liquid and store it in their stomachs. Once the bees are loaded up with nectar, they return home.

Bees live in large groups called colonies, and their home is known as a hive. When bees get back to the hive, they unload the nectar from their stomachs into small compartments that they've built from wax. (The bees make their own wax, too!) The nectar mixes with substances from the bee's own body, and after about five days it thickens into honey. Then it's ready to eat.

But nectar isn't the only thing bees get from flowers. Bees also eat pollen, and when they visit flowers, they're on the lookout for that, too. They store the tiny pollen grains in sacks behind their legs to bring back to the hive. But as they fly around, they also spread pollen to other flowers. That's how the plants are pollinated, allowing them to bear fruit. Apples, pears, peaches, almonds, and cantaloupes are just some of the delicious foods that bees help make possible.

And what about those painful bee stings? A bee sting is no fun, but it hurts the bee a lot more than it hurts you. Once a bee stings someone, it dies. So rest assured, bees only sting people when they feel threatened. If you don't bother them, they won't bother you. All in all, bees are amazing insects—not a pain at all!

Busy Bees

Comprehension Check

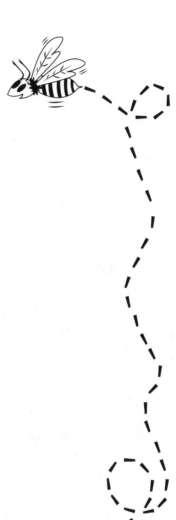

1. When do bees collect nectar?

_____

2. Where do bees find nectar?
- Ⓐ inside flowers
- Ⓑ in their stomachs
- Ⓒ in the hive
- Ⓓ in sacks behind their legs

3. What is the name for a group of bees?

_____

4 What happens when pollen spreads to flowers?
- Ⓐ It makes a big mess.
- Ⓑ Honey is formed.
- Ⓒ The plants are pollinated.
- Ⓓ The bees make wax.

5. How does the author of this passage feel about bees? How do you know?

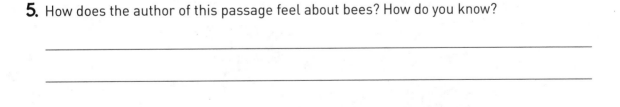

Name _____   Date _____

Busy Bees

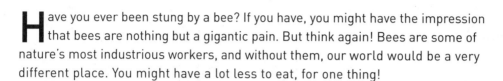

Have you ever been stung by a bee? If you have, you might have the impression that bees are nothing but a gigantic pain. But think again! Bees are some of nature's most industrious workers, and without them, our world would be a very different place. You might have a lot less to eat, for one thing!

That honey on your toast? You have bees to thank for it. During the spring and summer, female bees flit from flower to flower, gathering nectar from deep inside the blossoms. (Only females gather nectar. Male bees, known as "drones" have no role in honey production.) The bees extract the nectar from the flowers and store it in their stomachs. Once they're loaded up, they make the return flight home.

Bees live in large groups called colonies, and their communal home is known as a hive. When a female bee returns after a day of foraging, she unloads the syrupy liquid from her stomach into small, perfectly hexagonal compartments made of wax, called a honeycomb. (Believe it or not, the bees make their own wax, known as "beeswax"!) The nectar mixes with enzymes—special proteins from the bee's body— and after about five days, the mixture thickens into honey and is ready to eat. Bees eat the honey, and we do, too.

Gathering nectar isn't the only thing those bees are doing in the garden. They're also collecting pollen, a powdery substance produced by plants, which they bring back to the hive to eat. They store the tiny pollen grains in sacks behind their legs, but as they fly, some of the pollen floats away and spreads to other flowers. This is how the plants are pollinated, allowing them to bear fruit. Apples, pears, peaches, almonds, and cantaloupes are just some of the delicious foods that bees help bring to your table.

And what about those painful bee stings? A bee sting is no fun, but it hurts the bee a lot more than it hurts you. Once a bee stings someone, it dies. So rest assured, bees only sting people when they feel threatened. As a rule of thumb, if you don't bother them, they won't bother you. All in all, bees are amazing insects—not a pain at all!

Busy Bees

Comprehension Check

1. Why does the author say you should thank bees for the honey on your toast?

_____

_____

2. Do male or female bees gather nectar?

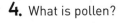

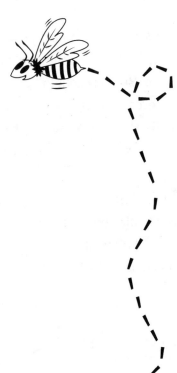

3. According to the passage, what are enzymes?

   Ⓐ hexagonal compartments

   Ⓑ special proteins from a bee's body

   Ⓒ honeycombs

   Ⓓ communal homes

4. What is pollen?

   Ⓐ a powdery substance that plants produce

   Ⓑ an ingredient in honey

   Ⓒ the place where bees live

   Ⓓ a kind of fruit

5. What is the main idea of this passage?

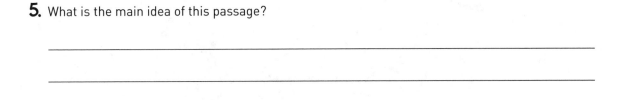

_____

_____

_____

Bobbie the Wonder Dog

This is a true story of a pooch named Bobbie. He did something pretty amazing. When people heard his story, they called him "Wonder Dog."

In 1923 an Oregon family took a car trip to Indiana. They went to visit relatives. They brought their dog, Bobbie, along on the trip. While they were in Indiana, Bobbie got away. The family looked for him everywhere. But he was lost! Finally they went home without him. They were heart-broken. They thought they would never see him again.

But they were wrong. Nine months later, a dog showed up at their house. They looked at the dog. They wondered where he'd come from. He looked like Bobbie. But they couldn't believe it was him. Then they saw that the dog had three scars, just like Bobbie. It really *was* Bobbie! He was dirty and smelly. His paws were raw. He had lost a lot of weight and was very tired. And no wonder! Bobbie had walked 2,700 miles!

People heard Bobbie's amazing tale. His story was in the news. A movie was even made about him. People called him Bobbie the Wonder Dog. He was famous! He might have liked being a movie star. But he was definitely happy to be back home.

Bobbie the Wonder Dog

Comprehension Check

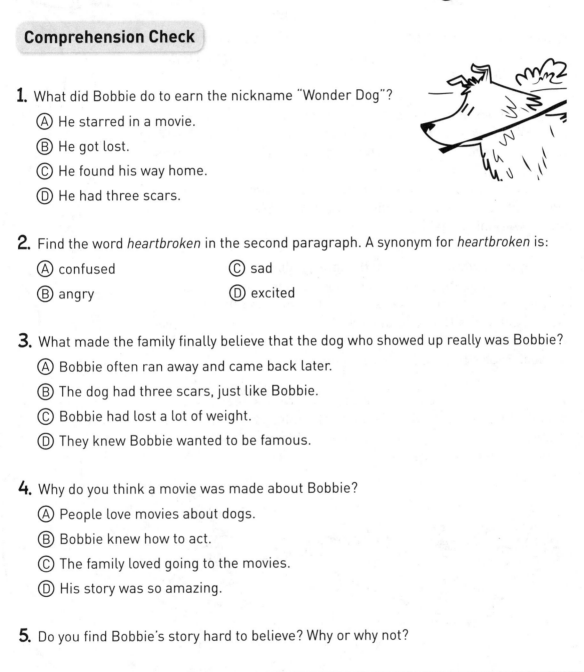

1. What did Bobbie do to earn the nickname "Wonder Dog"?

   Ⓐ He starred in a movie.

   Ⓑ He got lost.

   Ⓒ He found his way home.

   Ⓓ He had three scars.

2. Find the word *heartbroken* in the second paragraph. A synonym for *heartbroken* is:

   Ⓐ confused   Ⓒ sad

   Ⓑ angry   Ⓓ excited

3. What made the family finally believe that the dog who showed up really was Bobbie?

   Ⓐ Bobbie often ran away and came back later.

   Ⓑ The dog had three scars, just like Bobbie.

   Ⓒ Bobbie had lost a lot of weight.

   Ⓓ They knew Bobbie wanted to be famous.

4. Why do you think a movie was made about Bobbie?

   Ⓐ People love movies about dogs.

   Ⓑ Bobbie knew how to act.

   Ⓒ The family loved going to the movies.

   Ⓓ His story was so amazing.

5. Do you find Bobbie's story hard to believe? Why or why not?

_____

_____

_____

Bobbie the Wonder Dog

Most dogs are pretty smart. But some dogs, like Bobbie the Wonder Dog, are just plain amazing. This is a true story of a dog who accomplished a feat most *people* probably never could.

In 1923 Bobbie went on a long car trip with his owners. The family drove all the way from Oregon to Indiana. At the end of their trip, when they were ready to return home, they realized Bobbie was missing! They looked everywhere, but he was nowhere to be found. Even though Bobbie was like a member of the family, they had no choice but to return home without him. They were sure they would never see Bobbie again.

But they were wrong. Nine months later, a dog showed up at their house. They thought the dog resembled Bobbie, but they couldn't believe it was him. Then they saw that this dog had three scars, just like Bobbie. It really was him! He was dirty and smelly. His paws were raw. He had lost a lot of weight and was very tired. And no wonder! Bobbie had walked 2,700 miles!

When word got out, he became a celebrity. Newspapers everywhere told his story, and a movie was made about his long trip. Bobbie probably didn't care very much about being famous. He was likely just ecstatic to be back home.

Bobbie the Wonder Dog

Comprehension Check

1. In the first paragraph, what does the word *feat* mean?
   - (A) something that's difficult to do
   - (B) a long trip
   - (C) an amazing story
   - (D) the body part we walk on

2. Why did the family go home without Bobbie?
   - (A) Bobbie wanted to stay in Indiana.
   - (B) They were tired of him.
   - (C) They realized they never should have brought him.
   - (D) He was lost, and they couldn't find him.

3. When the dog showed up at their home, why didn't the family believe it was Bobbie?

   _____

   _____

4. In the last sentence *ecstatic* means:
   - (A) grateful
   - (B) tired
   - (C) very happy
   - (D) fearful

5. Do you think it's important to state at the beginning that this is a true story? Why or why not?

   _____

   _____

   _____

Bobbie the Wonder Dog

If you're a dog owner, you probably already know that dogs are pretty smart. But a few dogs—like Bobbie the Wonder Dog—are downright amazing. Bobbie was a scotch collie who lived in Oregon in the 1920s. He did something so extraordinary, he truly earned the title "Wonder Dog."

In the summer of 1923, Bobbie's owners took a car trip to visit relatives in Indiana, six states away. Since Bobbie was a part of family, they took him along. But when the family was ready to return home, they realized Bobbie was missing! They searched high and low, but nobody could find him. Finally they had to return home, heartbroken. They never expected to see Bobbie again.

Imagine their surprise when nine months later, Bobbie showed up on their doorstep! At first they weren't sure it was him. But this scrawny dog had three scars, in the very same places Bobbie did. They realized that this was indeed their beloved Bobbie. The dog was dirty, smelly, and his paws were raw. He'd lost weight and was exhausted. And with good reason; as far as anyone could figure out, Bobbie had walked 2,700 miles!

When word got out, he became a celebrity. Newspapers everywhere told his story. A movie was even made about his extraordinary trip. Bobbie probably didn't care very much for his newfound fame. After walking all that way, he was no doubt just happy to be back home.

Bobbie the Wonder Dog

Comprehension Check

1. In the second paragraph, what does the phrase "searched high and low" mean?

(A) searched on tiptoes and down on hands and knees

(B) looked everywhere

(C) looked at a map of the U.S.

(D) gave up searching

2. Why was the family heartbroken when they left Indiana?

_____

_____

3. A synonym for *scrawny* in paragraph 3 is:

(A) skinny

(B) shaggy

(C) muddy

(D) tired

4. In the last paragraph, what does the word *extraordinary* mean?

_____

5. What's the main idea of the last paragraph?

_____

_____

_____

Catching Zzzz's

Do you like to sleep? You certainly spend a lot of time doing it. Most kids your age sleep nine to ten hours every night. But have you ever wondered *why*?

Nearly all animals sleep. But some sleep a lot more than others. The brown bat, for instance, sleeps most of its life away. Every day it sleeps 19.9 hours. You might wonder how it gets anything else done! Giraffes don't sleep much at all. They sleep only about 1.9 hours each day.

Even ants sleep. Scientists studied them to find out. They found that worker ants took 250 naps a day. But each nap lasted only about a minute. The scientists added all the naps together. They found that the ants slept a total of 4 hours and 48 minutes per day.

So we know that most animals sleep. But why do they do it? Scientists aren't quite sure. But they do have some ideas.

One theory is that sleep gives our bodies a chance to recover after a day's work. Some activities, like muscle growth, take place when we're asleep.

Scientists also believe that we save energy when we sleep. This gives our brains a break. Experts think that the brain rests and rebuilds itself during sleep. Some believe that this "brain break" is the main function of sleep.

There's a lot about sleep that we still don't know. But one thing experts *do* know for sure is that sleep is good for you. If you went too long without sleep, you'd feel awful. So the next time your mom or dad says it's time for bed, smile, grab your p.j.'s, and say, "Give me some zzzz's, please."

Catching Zzzz's

Comprehension Check

1. According to the passage, how many hours each night do most kids sleep?

_____

2. Which animal sleeps 1.9 hours a day?

Ⓐ the giraffe   Ⓒ the worker ant

Ⓑ the brown bat   Ⓓ the brown ant

3. When does muscle growth take place?

Ⓐ in the morning

Ⓑ when people are young

Ⓒ during sleep

Ⓓ around the clock

4. Experts think our brains _____ during sleep.

Ⓐ get tired

Ⓑ use more energy

Ⓒ stop working

Ⓓ rest and rebuild themselves

5. According to the passage, if you went a long time without sleep, how would you feel?

Ⓐ excited

Ⓑ awful

Ⓒ hungry

Ⓓ happy

Catching Zzzz's

Every day you spend more time doing one activity than any other. What is it? Sleeping! If you're like most kids your age, you spend between nine and ten hours every night tucked in bed, sound asleep.

Almost all animals sleep, but the number of hours they do so varies widely. On one end of the sleep spectrum, there's the brown bat. It sleeps a total of 19.9 hours a day. You might wonder how it gets anything else done! Giraffes are at the other extreme. On average, they sleep a mere 1.9 hours each day. Apparently, a good night's sleep isn't necessary for growing tall!

Even ants sleep, but they do it in tiny, ant-size portions. Scientists found that worker ants took 250 naps a day, but each nap lasted only about a minute. The ants' sleep for the day totaled 4 hours and 48 minutes.

So, while some animals do more and some do less, they all sleep. But why? Even though scientists have been asking questions about sleep for decades, they still don't have a lot of answers. But they have some ideas.

One theory is that when we sleep, we give our bodies a chance to recover from all the work we did during the day. Certain activities like muscle growth take place when we're asleep.

Another theory is that it's the brain that really needs sleep. Energy is conserved when we sleep. As a result, our brains get a break. During sleep our brains have a chance to rest and regenerate themselves.

So there's still a lot left to discover about the mysterious activity of sleep. But one thing experts *can* say for sure is that sleep is very good for you. If you went too long without it, you'd feel truly miserable. So the next time your mom or dad says it's time for bed, smile, grab your p.j.'s, and say, "Give me some zzzz's, please."

Catching Zzzz's

Comprehension Check

1. What activity do most people spend the most time doing every day?

   _____

2. Based on this passage, do you think bigger animals need more sleep than smaller animals? What makes you think so?

   _____

   _____

   _____

3. How long is each ant-sized nap?
   (A) 250 seconds   (C) 4 hours
   (B) a minute   (D) 48 seconds

4. Tell one theory scientists have for why we sleep.
   (A) Scientist don't have any theories.
   (B) We are tired.
   (C) Sleep is mysterious.
   (D) Sleep gives our bodies a chance to recover.

5. In the last paragraph, why do you think sleep is referred to as "mysterious"
   (A) because it happens at night
   (B) because all animals sleep
   (C) because there's so much we don't understand about it
   (D) because energy is conserved when we sleep

Catching Zzzz's

Every day you spend more time doing one activity than any other. What is it? Sleeping! If you're like most kids your age, you spend between nine and ten hours every night tucked in bed sawing logs.

Scientists think almost all animals sleep, except perhaps a few rare species of fish, but the number of hours they sleep ranges widely. Take the brown bat, for instance. It sleeps a whopping 19.9 hours a day. You might wonder how it manages to get anything else done! Giraffes are at the other end of the sleep spectrum, snoozing a mere 1.9 hours each day. Apparently, sleep isn't a prerequisite for growing tall!

Even ants find time to sleep, albeit in tiny, ant-size portions. Scientists who studied them found that worker ants took 250 naps a day, but each nap lasted only about a minute. All told, the ants slept 4 hours and 48 minutes in one day.

So, while some animals do more of it and some do less, they all sleep. But why? Why do we humans spend a full *third* of our lives curled up in bed catching zzzz's? Although scientists have been puzzling with questions about sleep for several decades, they still don't have a whole lot of answers. But they do have some ideas.

When it comes to why we sleep, one theory is that sleep gives our bodies a chance to recover from all the work we did during the day. Certain biological activities, such as muscle growth, take place only when we're sleeping. Scientists also believe that energy is conserved when we sleep, and so another theory suggests that sleep provides our brains with a chance to rest and regenerate themselves.

Another question sleep experts haven't figured out is why we dream, but they think everyone does it for two hours or more every night—even though we don't always remember our dreams in the morning.

So there's still a lot left to discover about sleep, but one thing experts *can* say for sure is that sleep is good for you. If you went too long without it, you'd feel truly miserable. So the next time your mom or dad says it's time for bed, smile, grab your p.j.'s, and say, "Give me some zzzz's, please."

Catching Zzzz's

Comprehension Check

1. In paragraph 1, the phrase "sawing logs" is an idiom. What does it mean?

_____

2. Which is a synonym for the word *albeit* (pronounced *all-be-it*), used in paragraph 3?

   Ⓐ unless   Ⓒ of course

   Ⓑ although   Ⓓ anyway

3. Tell one theory scientists have to explain why we sleep.

_____

_____

_____

4. According to the passage, what haven't sleep experts figured out about dreaming?

   Ⓐ how many hours we dream each night

   Ⓑ why we dream

   Ⓒ why our dreams are so crazy

   Ⓓ who dreams and who doesn't

5. Which of the following can you infer from this passage?

   Ⓐ Scientists will probably stop studying sleep.

   Ⓑ Scientists will continue to study sleep to find more answers.

   Ⓒ Scientists think sleep is a boring topic.

   Ⓓ Scientists will solve the mysteries of sleep very soon.

Nightlights That Fly!

Have you ever seen a firefly? If you have, you know how cool they are. But lots of people have never seen one. That's because fireflies live only in certain parts of the country. And they have very short lives. Most fireflies live for just a week or two.

Another name for fireflies is "lightning bugs." These insects are really a kind of beetle. Fireflies are nocturnal. That means they're active at night. If you saw one during the day, you might not notice it. But at night, fireflies do something special. They glow!

Fireflies glow to attract a mate. They use their lights to talk to each other. Males and females flash signals back and forth. Each firefly species has its own way of flashing lights. A female looks for the flash from a male of the same species. When she sees it, she flashes back. This is how they "talk" to each other.

The glow also plays another role. It helps to keep predators away. Fireflies' bodies are filled with a bitter chemical that tastes really bad. If a predator eats a firefly, it's not too happy about it. The next time the predator sees a firefly's glow, it remembers the terrible taste. And it leaves the firefly alone.

Lucky for us! Fireflies don't glow just to look cool. But we can enjoy the show all the same.

That flash looks great on you.

Nightlights That Fly!

Comprehension Check

1. What is another name for fireflies?

_____

2. Why have some people never seen a firefly?
- (A) because they only come out at night
- (B) because they are very small
- (C) because they come out in the summer
- (D) because they only live in certain parts of the country

3. Why do fireflies glow?
- (A) to fly faster
- (B) to attract a mate
- (C) to scare people
- (D) because they're special

4. What does the word *predator* mean in paragraph 4?
- (A) an animal that eats another animal
- (B) a friend
- (C) a different species of firefly
- (D) a lightning bug

5. What are fireflies' bodies filled with?

_____

Nightlights That Fly!

Have you ever seen a firefly? If you have, you're lucky. Many people have never spotted one. These amazing insects are found only in certain regions. In the United States, they're generally seen in the eastern and southern states. People usually spy them in June and July. But their lives are short. Once they take flight, they live for only a week or two.

Fireflies are also known as "lightning bugs." These nocturnal insects are actually a kind of beetle. If you saw one during the day, it might look like an ordinary beetle. But at night, when they're active, these amazing insects glow. They're nightlights that fly!

The main reason a firefly glows is to attract a mate. Males and females of the same species flash signals back and forth as a way of talking to each other. Each firefly species has its own particular pattern. When a female recognizes the flash from a male of the same species, she answers back with her own flash. Ah, true love!

The glow serves another purpose, as well. It helps keep predators away. Fireflies' bodies are filled with a bitter chemical that tastes awful. If a predator eats a firefly, it's not too happy. The next time the predator sees a firefly's glow, it remembers the terrible taste. And it leaves the firefly alone.

Lucky for us! Fireflies may not be glowing on summer nights for our benefit, but we can enjoy them all the same.

That flash looks great on you.

Nightlights That Fly!

Comprehension Check

1. Which word in paragraph 2 means "active at night"?

_____

2. Fireflies are actually a kind of

Ⓐ lightning bug.

Ⓑ beetle.

Ⓒ nightlight.

Ⓓ chemical.

3. Why do male and female fireflies flash signals to each other?

_____

_____

4. In addition to attracting a mate, what other purpose does the glowing serve?

_____

_____

5. Why does the author write "Lucky for us!" in the last paragraph?

_____

_____

_____

Nightlights That Fly!

Have you ever seen a firefly? If you have, you're lucky. Many people have never glimpsed one because these wondrous insects are found only in certain regions and live for a very brief time. In the United States, fireflies (also known as "lightning bugs") are generally found in the eastern and southern states. The first ones are usually spotted in June, and by August, they're usually all gone.

There are more than 1,900 different species of fireflies, and all are actually a kind of beetle. But fireflies are no ordinary beetle. What makes them truly special is that they glow. The question most people ask is *why?*

As it turns out, the main reason a firefly glows is to attract a mate. Males and females of the same species flash signals back and forth as a way of communicating. Each firefly species has its own particular "language," a pattern of flashes unique to them. When a female recognizes the flash from a male of the same species, she answers back with her own flash. Ah, true love!

A firefly's glow gives it an added advantage. It enables it to stave off predators. Fireflies' bodies are filled with a chemical that tastes so bitter that any predator that tastes it once, will never want to taste it again! Because of a firefly's glow, predators learn to associate the glow with this terrible taste. And so they leave the fireflies alone.

Lucky for us! Fireflies may have their own reasons for glowing, but for a few fleeting weeks each summer, we get to enjoy the show!

That flash looks great on you.

Name _____ Date _____

Nightlights That Fly!

Comprehension Check

1. What does the word *glimpsed* mean in paragraph 1? What's another word in that paragraph that means the same thing?

_____

2. According to the passage, why are fireflies "no ordinary beetle"?

_____

3. What does each firefly species have?

_____

_____

4. What does the phrase "stave off" mean in paragraph 4?

Ⓐ attract
Ⓑ keep away
Ⓒ kill
Ⓓ confuse

5. How does the author feel about fireflies? How do you know?

_____

_____

_____

"Dear Aunt Edna . . ."

Let's say you wanted to send a message to your Aunt Edna. You could send an e-mail. You could send a text message. Or you could send an instant message. What do all of these have in common? They're fast!

Sending written messages is nothing new. But the way we send them and how soon they get there are very new. Lately delivering messages has gotten very fast.

It wasn't always this way. In colonial days, mail delivery was slow. It took a long time to receive a letter. At first, *merchants*, or shopkeepers, delivered mail when they traveled. Later, postal carriers did it. But they didn't follow a schedule. And they traveled alone on horseback. It could take a month or more for mail to get from one colony to another. Talk about snail mail!

In the following years the country grew. And so did mail delivery. New roads were built. New kinds of transportation were used. These helped keep the mail moving.

Today mail is carried in trucks. And sometimes it's carried in airplanes. But even airmail is slow compared to the fast messages we have today. These arrive in almost no time. Today, you don't have to wait. When you want to get a message to someone *right this second* . . . you can!

TO: jk56

Hi Send Cancel

"Dear Aunt Edna . . ."

Comprehension Check

1. According to the passage, what do e-mails, text messages, and instant messages all have in common?

_____

2. In colonial days, mail delivery was

   Ⓐ faster than it is today.

   Ⓑ once a week.

   Ⓒ slow.

   Ⓓ in the morning.

3. A merchant is a

   Ⓐ shopkeeper.

   Ⓑ banker.

   Ⓒ sailor.

   Ⓓ writer.

4. According to paragraph 4, the new forms of transportation

   Ⓐ cost a lot of money.

   Ⓑ were very exciting.

   Ⓒ kept the mail moving.

   Ⓓ made no difference to mail delivery.

5. According to the passage, what are two ways mail is now carried?

_____

"Dear Aunt Edna . . ."

Today, you can communicate with your friends and family at lightning speed. You can e-mail, twitter, and instant message people all over the world. You can even send a quick to note to your Aunt Edna, thanking her for your birthday present. Messages can be received in seconds. But it wasn't always this way. In fact, today's instant communication has been around only since the 1990s.

Sending written messages, of course, is nothing new. Egyptians were the first to do it. Way back in 2400 BC, foot messengers carried news from the rulers. Traveling on foot could take quite a while. But the messages eventually reached their recipients.

In this country, too, mail once took a long time to get where it was going. In early colonial days, friends and merchants delivered mail. Later, postal carriers did the job. But they didn't follow a schedule. They traveled on horseback, and the roads were poor. That meant it could take a month or more for mail to get from one colony to another.

In the following years the country expanded. And so did mail delivery. Roads were built, and new methods of transportation were used. These helped get the mail from here to there. Message delivery started out on foot, and ended up in trucks, trains, and airplanes.

But even airmail is slow compared to the instant messages we have today. These arrive in almost no time. Today, you don't have to wait. When you want to get a message to someone *right this second* . . . you can!

"Dear Aunt Edna . . ."

Comprehension Check

1. According to the passage, what happened in the 1990s?

_____

_____

2. How were the first written messages delivered?

Ⓐ by messengers on horseback

Ⓑ by messengers on foot

Ⓒ by telegraph

Ⓓ by word of mouth

3. How were letters delivered in early colonial times?

Ⓐ by messengers on horseback

Ⓑ by boat

Ⓒ by family members

Ⓓ by traveling friends and merchants

4. A person who receives a letter or message is the

Ⓐ recipient

Ⓑ sender

Ⓒ postal carrier

Ⓓ messenger

5. In the last paragraph, why does the author say that airmail is slow?

_____

_____

"Dear Aunt Edna . . ."

There was once a time when it took weeks or months to get a message to someone who lived far away—like your Aunt Edna, for instance. You might find that hard to believe. Today you can text, e-mail, twitter, and instant message people all over the globe. Messages can be sent in seconds. But it wasn't always this way. In fact, super-fast communication is very new.

The wish to share written messages probably goes all the way back to the invention of writing itself. Historians say the first system to deliver written messages dates back to ancient Egypt. In 2400 BC, couriers—or foot messengers—carried decrees from the pharaohs. It could take quite a while for these messages to reach their recipients.

In the early days of this country, mail was just as slow. In colonial times, travelers delivered mail for people. Later, postal carriers took on the job. But mail was still delivered haphazardly. Postal carriers didn't follow a schedule. They waited until they had enough mail to make a trip worthwhile. They traveled on horseback, and the roads were poor. It could take a month or more for mail to get from Massachusetts to Virginia.

Over the years, as the country grew, people found new and faster ways to deliver mail. They built roads and used new methods of transportation to get the mail from here to there. Message delivery started out on foot, but it progressed to stagecoaches, trucks, trains, and airplanes.

In the 1990s, things sped up even more. Even airmail is slow compared to instant messages, which arrive at their destinations instantaneously. Today, when you want to get a message to someone far away *right this second* . . . you can!

"Dear Aunt Edna . . ."

Comprehension Check

1. Who had the first system of message delivery?

_____

2. What does the word *haphazardly* mean in paragraph 3?

Ⓐ randomly; in a disorganized way

Ⓑ on time

Ⓒ slowly

Ⓓ coming very quickly

3. According to the passage, what happened as the country grew?

Ⓐ Mail delivery became more haphazard.

Ⓑ People stopped sending mail.

Ⓒ New methods of transportation were used to carry mail.

Ⓓ Postal carriers had to work longer hours.

4. When did super-fast communication begin?

_____

5. Based on this passage, what's the main way the new forms of messaging are different from the older forms?

_____

Practice, Practice, Practice . . . Makes Perfect!

What do you think it takes to become great at something? Do you believe that some talented people are born that way? Do you think others are born with no talent at all? Here's a secret: *When it comes to getting good at anything, the most important part is practice.*

That's right. Practice. A lot of it.

Many people think that talent is the only thing that counts. They think that greatness is "born, not made." In this view, some people are just born with more ability than everybody else. And that's that.

Of course, some people do have more natural ability than others. And some people have less. But talent alone doesn't make someone great. And people with less talent can *become* great. How? By putting in the time practicing. How much time? One researcher says it takes about ten thousand hours. That's a lot of practice!

You might think ten thousand hours sounds impossible. But it's really about ten or twelve years of steady practice. So you've got plenty of time to get good at the thing you love doing.

It really helps if you enjoy the activity. Then you'll want to spend a lot of doing it. You'll probably never be able to spend ten thousand hours practicing the piano if you'd really rather play the drums. But if nothing makes you happier than hitting a tennis ball with a racket or sitting in your room doing math equations, the more time you spend doing it, the better you'll get. Guaranteed!

Practice, Practice, Practice . . . Makes Perfect!

Comprehension Check

1. What is the secret given in the first paragraph?
   Ⓐ Practice is the most important part of getting good at something.
   Ⓑ Some people are born with lots of talent.
   Ⓒ It's easy to be great at something.
   Ⓓ Some people are born with no talent at all.

2. According to one researcher, how long does it take to get really good at something?

   _____

3. Ten thousand hours is about how many years of steady practice?

   _____

4. Why is it easier to get good at something you enjoy?
   Ⓐ If you like doing something, you'll want to spend more time doing it.
   Ⓑ If you like doing something, you don't have to practice.
   Ⓒ Playing the piano is hard.
   Ⓓ Fun activities are always easy.

5. What is the main idea of this passage?
   Ⓐ Some people will never be good at anything.
   Ⓑ To be great at something, you have to practice a lot.
   Ⓒ Some people with a lot of talent, don't have to practice.
   Ⓓ Practice is boring.

Practice, Practice, Practice . . . Makes Perfect!

Have you ever heard someone say, "Practice, practice, practice"? When people say this, they're conveying the idea that getting really good at something doesn't happen overnight. It takes a *lot* of practice.

So how do you become the best you can be when it comes to playing the piano or scoring goals in soccer? The answer, if you haven't guessed, is practice! A lot of it.

Many people think that talent is the most important ingredient in high achievement. They think that greatness is "born, not made." In this view, some people are just born with more talent than everybody else. And that's that the end of the story.

Recently, though, people have been challenging this idea. Of course, some people do have more natural ability than others. But talent by itself doesn't make someone great. And people with less talent can *become* great. The most important factor in being a high achiever is putting in the time practicing. How much time? One researcher says it takes about ten thousand hours. That's a lot of practice!

You might think ten thousand hours sounds impossible. But it's really about ten or twelve years of steady practice. So you've got plenty of time to get good at the thing you love doing.

It really helps if you enjoy the activity. Then you'll be motivated to put in a lot of time. You'll probably never be able to spend ten thousand hours practicing the piano if you'd really rather play the drums. But if nothing makes you happier than whacking a tennis ball with a racket or sitting in your room doing math equations, the more time you spend doing it, the better you'll get. Guaranteed!

Practice, Practice, Practice . . . Makes Perfect!

Comprehension Check

1. People who think that greatness is "born, not made" believe

   Ⓐ anyone can be great at something.

   Ⓑ practice is hard work.

   Ⓒ only people born with a lot of talent can be great at something.

   Ⓓ practice makes perfect.

2. A synonym for *talent* is

   Ⓐ muscle.   Ⓒ strength.

   Ⓑ natural ability.   Ⓓ passion.

3. According to the passage, which of these is true?

   Ⓐ Talent alone doesn't make someone great at something.

   Ⓑ Talent is really all that counts.

   Ⓒ People with natural ability don't have to practice.

   Ⓓ Hard work is pointless.

4. According to the passage, how many hours of practice does it take to get really good at something?

   _____

5. In the last paragraph, what does the word *motivated* mean?

   Ⓐ feeling pressure from others

   Ⓑ having a desire to do something

   Ⓒ too tired

   Ⓓ upset

Practice, Practice, Practice . . . Makes Perfect!

There's a famous old joke that goes like this: A tourist visiting New York City stops a man on the street and asks, "How do you get to Carnegie Hall?" The man replies, "Practice, practice, practice!"

The joke is funny (to some people, anyway!) because the tourist isn't asking how to become a great musician—someone who might one day be good enough to play at the famous concert hall. The tourist just wants to know if he should turn right or left.

But the man's answer—"Practice, practice, practice!"—is good advice for anyone who wants to get really good at something. If you want to become the best you can be when it comes to playing the violin, painting portraits, or scoring goals in soccer, your best bet is to practice— a lot.

Many people think that accomplished artists, athletes, and scientists—amazing musicians like Mozart or tennis greats like Venus and Serena Williams—just have more talent and natural ability than everybody else. But others point out that the truth is more complicated. Of course those people have loads of talent. But talent by itself doesn't make someone great. The most important ingredient in being a high achiever is putting in the time. How much time? One researcher speculates it takes about ten thousand hours.

Ten thousand hours sounds like a lot, but it's basically about ten or twelve years of steady practice. It helps if you enjoy the activity, because then you'll be motivated to put in a lot of time. You'll probably never be able to spend ten thousand hours practicing the piano if you'd really rather play the drums. But if nothing makes you happier than whacking a tennis ball with a racket or sitting in your room doing math equations, the more time you spend doing it, the better you'll get. Guaranteed! And if piano is your true love, you might even end up at Carnegie Hall.

Practice, Practice, Practice . . . Makes Perfect!

Comprehension Check

1. What is Carnegie Hall?
   - (A) a famous concert hall in New York City
   - (B) a place in New York City where people often get lost
   - (C) a place where people tell jokes
   - (D) a restaurant that tourists often go to

2. According to the passage, what is the best way to be the best you can be at something?

   _____

3. Why does the author mention Mozart and Venus and Serena Williams in paragraph 4?

   _____

   _____

4. What does the word *speculates* mean in paragraph 4?
   - (A) hopes
   - (B) forgets
   - (C) promises
   - (D) supposes

5. Based on the passage, do you think talent is completely unimportant? Why or why not?

   _____

   _____

   _____

Lonesome George: The Last of His Kind

The Galapagos Islands are an island chain off the coast of Ecuador in South America. One of these islands is named Pinta. For a long time, Pinta was home to a kind of tortoise known as the Pinta Island tortoise.

Pinta had lots of these tortoises. But over the years, people hunted them. Now, they are almost extinct. In fact, there is just one left! His name is George, and he's nearly 100 years old. People call him Lonesome George. Why? Because he's the last of his kind.

Scientists hope that George will become a dad before he dies. If he does, then he will pass on his genes. And the Pinta Island tortoise won't die out.

Even though George is old, he still has time. Some Pinta Island tortoises live to be 150. The real problem is finding George a mate. There are no females left. But some other tortoises are very closely related. Scientists hope George will mate with one of them.

George may not know it, but he has become famous. There are a lot of people rooting for him. They hope that he will pass on his genes so that Pinta Island tortoises will live on. Then George won't be lonesome anymore.

Lonesome George: The Last of His Kind

Comprehension Check

1. Where are the Galapagos Islands?

    Ⓐ off the coast of Ecuador in South America

    Ⓑ near Chile in South America

    Ⓒ near Pinta Island

    Ⓓ in North America

2. What kind of animal is Lonesome George?

    _____

3. Why is George nicknamed "Lonesome George"

    Ⓐ because other tortoises ignore him

    Ⓑ because he is shy

    Ⓒ because he is the last Pinta Island tortoise in the world

    Ⓓ because he is unfriendly to other Pinta tortoises

4. How long do some tortoises live?

    _____

5. Why are people hoping George becomes a dad before he dies?

    Ⓐ If he has babies, the Pinta Island tortoises won't die out.

    Ⓑ They think George would make a great dad.

    Ⓒ They're hoping they can have one of the baby tortoises as a pet.

    Ⓓ They think baby tortoises are cute.

Lonesome George: The Last of His Kind

The Galapagos Islands are an island chain in South America. This group of islands is located off the coast of Ecuador. On one of these islands lives a very old tortoise named George. He's known by most everyone as "Lonesome George."

Lonesome George comes from the island of Pinta and is a Pinta Island tortoise. This is a *subspecies*, or subgroup, of the Galapagos Island tortoise. Why exactly is George so lonesome? He's the last living tortoise of his kind.

Once, Pinta Island was crawling with tortoises like George. But over hundreds of years, they became more and more scarce. For many years they were hunted and used for food and oil. Today, George is the last Pinta Island tortoise in the world. The *Guinness Book of World Records* has named him "the rarest living creature."

Scientists are hoping that George will mate before he dies. If he passes on his genes, the Pinta Island tortoises won't die out. George is nearly 100 years old. But Galapagos tortoises can live up to 150 years. So there's still time.

The problem has been finding George a mate. There are no female Pinta Island tortoises left. But there are two other types of tortoise that are very closely related. If George mates with one of these other subspecies, he can pass on his genes. But so far no offspring have been born.

George may not know it, but there are a lot of people rooting for him. They hope he'll find a mate. Then he won't be lonesome George anymore.

Lonesome George: The Last of His Kind

Comprehension Check

1. What is an island chain?

   Ⓐ a place in Ecuador

   Ⓑ a group of islands

   Ⓒ a place in South America

   Ⓓ an island that is round

2. Why is George called "Lonesome George"?

   _____

   _____

3. What is a subspecies?

   Ⓐ a large species

   Ⓑ a smaller group within a species

   Ⓒ a species that can swim

   Ⓓ a kind of tortoise that grows very old

4. What happened to the Pinta Island tortoises to cause them to disappear?

   Ⓐ They were hunted for many years.

   Ⓑ They found better places to live.

   Ⓒ They ran out of food.

   Ⓓ No one knows what happened to them.

5. Why are people hoping that George passes on his genes?

   _____

   _____

Name _____ Date _____

Lonesome George: The Last of His Kind

Lonesome George just might be the most famous tortoise in the world. George lives on the island of Santa Cruz, one of the Galapagos islands off the coast of Ecuador. He's originally from the island of Pinta, another island in the chain. George is estimated to be between 90 and 100 years old. And he weighs nearly 200 pounds. But those aren't the reasons he's famous.

George has become a celebrity because he's the last living Pinta Island tortoise in the world. Pinta Island tortoises are a subspecies of the giant Galapagos tortoise. If George doesn't have offspring before he dies, his subspecies will become extinct. The *Guinness Book of World Records* has declared George "the rarest living creature."

At nearly 100 years old, time would seem to be running out for old George. But by Galapagos tortoise standards, he's actually still in his prime. The tortoises can live up to 150 years. So there's still plenty of time for George to find a mate and reproduce.

The problem has been locating a mate. Although there are no remaining female Pinta Island tortoises, there are two other subspecies of tortoise in the Galapagos that are very closely related. Conservationists have been trying to encourage George to mate with one of these other subspecies so that he can pass on his genes. But so far no luck.

Hundreds of years ago, George's ancestors lived on Pinta Island in large numbers. But over the centuries they were hunted for food and oil, and eventually their numbers were all but wiped out. Now the future of these tortoises rests entirely on George's lonesome shoulders. People all over the world are rooting for him. They want George to have a family so he won't be so lonesome anymore.

Lonesome George: The Last of His Kind

Comprehension Check

1. Why has Lonesome George become famous?

_____

_____

2. What does the word *extinct* mean in paragraph 2?

_____

3. The word *subspecies* is formed by adding the prefix *sub-* to the word *species*. What do you think *subspecies* means?

_____

_____

4. What happened to George's ancestors?

_____

_____

5. What does the author mean when she writes "the future of the tortoises rests entirely on George's lonesome shoulders"?

_____

_____

_____

Gimme a Slice!

Do you like pizza? Do you know anyone who *doesn't*?! Americans are crazy about pizza pie. But did you know that pizza has been around for a very long time?

In fact, historians think that it goes back thousands of years. The first pizzas weren't like our pizzas today. They were flat pieces of bread. People baked them on cooking stones. These pizzas were plain. They didn't have cheese. And they didn't have fancy toppings.

Modern pizza began in the city of Naples in Italy. In the 1700s, Naples was very poor. Pizza became popular because it was cheap. People didn't have to buy a whole pie. They could just buy part of the pizza. Today, many places still sell pizza by the slice.

After a while, people in other parts of Italy tried it. And they liked it, too. It was no longer just for the poor. Even kings and queens ate it. Eventually it became one of Italy's national foods.

Americans first tasted pizza when people from Italy came to this country. Italians brought their favorite foods. And pizza was one of them. It became even more popular here after World War II. American soldiers who had been in Italy fell in love with pizza. When they came home, they wanted more. And word spread. Pretty soon, everybody else wanted a slice, too.

Gimme a Slice!

Comprehension Check

1. How were the first pizzas different from pizza today?

Ⓐ They were square instead of round.

Ⓑ They didn't have cheese or toppings.

Ⓒ The crust was very chewy.

Ⓓ They were served cold.

2. Where did the modern pizza get its start?

_____

3. Originally pizza was eaten by

Ⓐ the poor

Ⓑ by everybody

Ⓒ by people with big appetites

Ⓓ by kings and queens

4. When did pizza become popular in the United States?

Ⓐ in the 1700s

Ⓑ thousands of years ago

Ⓒ after World War II

Ⓓ after it became Italy's national food

5. What is the author's main purpose for writing this passage?

Ⓐ to persuade you that pizza is the best food

Ⓑ to describe her favorite pizza

Ⓒ to show the reasons people love pizza

Ⓓ to give a brief history of pizza

Name _____ Date _____

Gimme a Slice!

Do you like pizza? Do you know anyone who *doesn't*?! Americans, young and old, are crazy about pizza pie. And they have been for generations.

Pizza in some form has been around for a very long time. Historians think it goes back to the earliest civilizations. In early times, large, flat pieces of bread were baked on cooking stones. But the first pizzas didn't have cheese or toppings.

Modern pizza began in the Italian city of Naples. In the 1700s, pizza was a cheap food that was eaten by the poor. Often people didn't buy a whole pizza. They would buy only what they could afford. Today, many pizzerias still sell pizza by the slice. So it's still affordable for just about anyone.

Over time, pizza spread beyond Naples to the rest of Italy. And soon it became popular all over. Everyone ate it, even kings and queens. Different regions had their own favorite toppings. In time, it became one of Italy's national foods.

Today the cheesy pies are loved by Americans almost as much as Italians. Italian immigrants first introduced pizza to the States when they came to this country. Then after World War II, its popularity really grew. During the war, American soldiers in Italy ate a lot of pizza. And they loved it. When they came home, they wanted more. Word spread. And pretty soon, everybody else wanted a slice, too.

Gimme a Slice!

Comprehension Check

1. According to the passage, what got its start in Naples, Italy?

_____

2. Why was pizza eaten by the poor people of Naples?

_____

_____

3. According the passage, which is true?

Ⓐ Pizza is eaten only by young people.

Ⓑ Pizza is still affordable for most people.

Ⓒ A slice of pizza costs a lot these days.

Ⓓ Kings and queens hate pizza.

4. Pizza was introduced in the United States by

Ⓐ soldiers after World War II

Ⓑ kings and queens

Ⓒ the earliest civilizations

Ⓓ Italian immigrants

5. Why did pizza become popular in the United States after World War II?

Ⓐ It was cheap to make.

Ⓑ You could buy it by the slice.

Ⓒ American soldiers returning from Italy loved it, and the word spread.

Ⓓ It was introduced by Italian immigrants after the World War II.

Gimme a Slice!

Ask three of your friends what their favorite food is, and at least one of them will probably say, "Pizza." Americans, young and old, are crazy about pizza pie, and they have been for generations. And what's not to love? Chewy dough, gooey cheese, your favorite topping? Grab some napkins and dig in!

Some version of pizza has been around for a very long time. Historians can trace it all the way back to earliest civilization, when large, flat pieces of bread were baked on cooking stones. But it took centuries before the arrival of the round cheesy pie we know and love today.

Modern pizza began in Italy. It was originally an inexpensive food eaten by the very poor in eighteenth-century Naples. Instead of buying a whole pizza, customers would buy only what they could afford. This custom of buying just part of a pizza lives on in many places today, where people order pizza by the slice.

One of the most popular pizza toppings in Naples was tomatoes. Back then, many Italians were afraid to eat tomatoes because they believed they were poisonous. But the poor couldn't always be so choosy. They went ahead and put tomatoes on their pizzas—and they lived to tell about it!

Over time, pizza's popularity spread beyond Naples to the rest of Italy. It began to be eaten by everybody, with a variety of different toppings. Eventually it became one of Italy's national foods.

Today pizza is loved by Americans almost as much as by Italians. Italian immigrants who came to this country in the early 1900s first introduced the pies. But it was after World War II that it's popularity really took hold. When American soldiers came home after being in Italy, they clamored for the pizzas they'd grown to love. And pretty soon, everybody else wanted a slice, too.

Gimme a Slice!

Comprehension Check

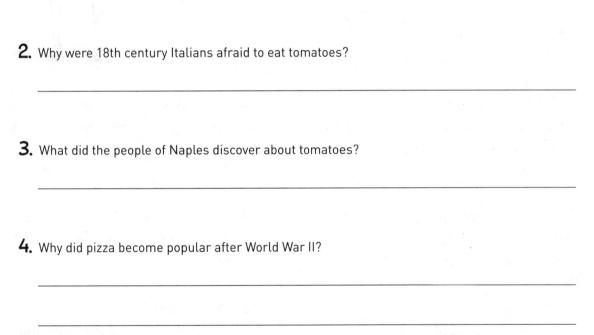

1. In paragraph 3, the word *custom* means

Ⓐ way of doing things

Ⓑ discovery

Ⓒ bargain

Ⓓ luck

2. Why were 18th century Italians afraid to eat tomatoes?

_____

3. What did the people of Naples discover about tomatoes?

_____

4. Why did pizza become popular after World War II?

_____

_____

5. A synonym for *clamored* in the last paragraph is

Ⓐ asked

Ⓑ cried out

Ⓒ whispered

Ⓓ hinted

What's the Point of Acupuncture?

If you were feeling sick or in pain, you might go to a doctor. She might tell you to rest. She might tell you to drink lots of fluids. But if you went to a doctor who practices *acupuncture* (ak-yoo-pungk-chur), she might do something very different. She might stick tiny needles in your body!

Acupuncture is a very old healing method that comes from China. Doctors in China have been using it on their patients for more than 2,000 years. But in the United States, acupuncture is still pretty new. Many Americans learned about it for the first time in the 1970s. That's when a man named James Reston wrote about it in *The New York Times*.

When Reston was in China, he had to have surgery. Afterward, his doctors treated him with acupuncture. They said it would help his pain. He didn't expect it to do much good. But the results surprised him. After the treatment he felt much better. He decided to write about it and share his story.

In the years since Reston's article, acupuncture has become more popular in the United States. It is said to be helpful for a lot of medical problems. But how exactly does it work? Many American doctors aren't sure.

Doctors who practice acupuncture believe the body contains an energy called *chi*. They say you can't see *chi*. But it is an energy that flows in the body. They believe that when the *chi* is flowing smoothly, the body is healthy. But when the *chi* gets stuck, the body gets sick or feels pain. They believe that sticking needles in the body gets the *chi* flowing again.

Do the needles hurt? They are very thin. Some are not much thicker than a strand of hair. Some people say they don't even feel them. Others say they feel a slight pinching, but it only lasts a few seconds. Fans of acupuncture say that the benefits are worth it. If a few needles can help get rid of aches and pains, they say, a little pinching is no big deal.

What's the Point of Acupuncture?

Comprehension Check

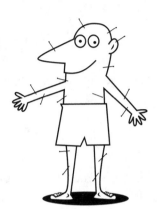

1. What is acupuncture?

Ⓐ a very old healing method from China

Ⓑ a system for drinking lots of fluids

Ⓒ a form of exercise

Ⓓ a kind of dance performance

2. When did many Americans first learn about acupuncture?

Ⓐ 2,000 years ago

Ⓑ in the 1970s

Ⓒ in the 1990s

Ⓓ in the 1800s

3. Doctors who practice acupuncture believe the body contains

Ⓐ an energy called *chi*.

Ⓑ a lot of energy.

Ⓒ aches and pains.

Ⓓ medical problems.

4. The needles used in acupuncture are

Ⓐ very cold.   Ⓒ very expensive.

Ⓑ very thin.   Ⓓ hard to find.

5. According to the passage, what is the purpose of acupuncture?

Ⓐ to get the *chi* flowing smoothly

Ⓑ to relax

Ⓒ to try something new

Ⓓ to teach people about different cultures

What's the Point of Acupuncture?

If you go to the doctor when you're sick or in pain, what does she do? She might tell you to rest and drink lots of fluids or give you some medicine. But she probably doesn't stick tiny needles in your body! Yet in an ancient practice from China called *acupuncture*, that's just what doctors do. And often, their patients feel better!

In China, acupuncture goes back thousands of years. But in the United States, it's still pretty new. Many Americans learned about it for the first time in the 1970s. That's when a writer named James Reston wrote about it in *The New York Times*.

When Reston was in China, he needed to have surgery. Afterward, he still had some pain. So his doctors treated him with acupuncture. To his surprise, after the treatment he felt much better. He was so impressed by the results that he wrote an article about his experience.

In the years since Reston's article, acupuncture has become more popular in the United States. It is said to be helpful for a range of conditions. But how exactly does it work? Many American doctors aren't quite sure.

Doctors who practice traditional Chinese medicine have different beliefs about the body than doctors have in this country. According to their view, the body contains an invisible energy called *chi*. They believe that when the *chi* is flowing smoothly, the body is healthy. But when the flow of *chi* is blocked, the body gets sick or feels pain.

They believe that by sticking very thin needles—some not much thicker than a strand of hair—into certain points on the body, the *chi* can be unblocked. Then it can flow freely again. And the pain or illness goes away.

Does acupuncture hurt? Some people say they don't even feel the needles. Others say they feel a slight pinching that lasts a few seconds. Fans of acupuncture say the benefits are worth it. If a few needles can help get rid of aches and pains, they say, a little pinching is no big deal.

What's the Point of Acupuncture?

Comprehension Check

1. If you went to a doctor who practices acupuncture, what would he or she do?

_____

_____

2. How long have doctors been practicing acupuncture in China?

_____

3. Why did James Reston write an article about acupuncture?

Ⓐ He thought it would be a fun subject to write about.

Ⓑ He was so impressed, he wanted to tell people about his experience.

Ⓒ He couldn't think of anything else to write about.

Ⓓ He wanted to be the first person to introduce it in the U.S.

4. According to the doctors who practice acupuncture, what happens when a person's *chi* is blocked?

_____

_____

5. Doctors who practice acupuncture have _____ than doctors have in this country.

Ⓐ different beliefs about the body

Ⓑ more patients

Ⓒ bigger offices

Ⓓ more books

What's the Point of Acupuncture?

If you had a runny nose or a pain in your knee, you probably wouldn't stick needles in your body and expect to feel better. But in an ancient practice from China known as *acupuncture*, this is exactly what doctors do to their patients. And often, their patients feel better!

Acupuncture has been practiced in China for thousands of years. But in the United States, it has only recently become popular. Many Americans learned about the practice for the first time in the 1970s. That's when a journalist named James Reston wrote about it when he was traveling in China.

In 1971 while visiting Peking, Reston needed to have an emergency surgery to remove his appendix. Afterward, his doctors treated him with acupuncture to manage some lingering pain. To his surprise, after the acupuncture he felt much better. He was so impressed by the results that he wrote about his experience in *The New York Times*.

In the years since Reston's article, acupuncture has become increasingly popular in the United States. It is said to be helpful for headaches and muscle strain, allergies and acne. But how exactly does it work? Many American doctors aren't quite sure.

Traditional Chinese medicine is founded on a philosophy of the body that's different from the one our doctors use. According to this ancient philosophy, the body contains an invisible energy known as *chi*. When the *chi* is flowing smoothly, the body is healthy, they believe. But when the flow of *chi* is blocked, the body experiences illness or pain.

By sticking very thin needles—some not much thicker than a strand of hair—into precise points on the body, acupuncturists say they unblock the *chi* so it can again flow freely. And then the pain or illness goes away.

Does acupuncture hurt? Some people say they don't even feel the needles. Others report a slight pinching that lasts a few seconds. Proponents of acupuncture say that the benefits are worth it. If a few needles can help relieve aches and pains, they say, a little pinching is no big deal.

What's the Point of Acupuncture?

Comprehension Check

1. In the practice of acupuncture doctors stick very thin needles in their patients. Why?

_____

_____

_____

2. According to the passage, how did many Americans first learn about acupuncture?

_____

_____

_____

3. Name two conditions that acupuncture is said to be helpful for?

_____

_____

4. What is the meaning of the word *philosophy* in paragraph 5?

   Ⓐ set of beliefs   Ⓒ computer

   Ⓑ book   Ⓓ language

5. In paragraph 6, the author compares the needle to a strand of hair. Why does she do this?

_____

_____

Pluto Gets Demoted

For years, our solar system had nine planets. But now there are only eight. What happened? Did one of the planets fall from the sky? Actually what happened is that astronomers changed their minds. For a long time they called Pluto a planet. Then in 2006, they decided it wasn't one. Pluto got demoted!

Problems for Pluto started in 2005. That year, astronomers discovered a dwarf planet named Eris, out beyond Pluto. The word dwarf means "smaller than normal." People were confused because Eris was *bigger* than Pluto. If Eris was only a dwarf planet, shouldn't Pluto be, too?

In 2006, a group of astronomers had a meeting. They decided to make some rules. They decided that before an object can be called a planet it has to pass three tests. If it passes all three, it's a planet. If it doesn't, then it's not.

First, the object has to *orbit*, or travel in a path, around the sun. *Check!* Pluto travels around the sun once every 248 years.

Second, it has to be big enough to form a round or nearly round shape. *Check!* Pluto is round like the other planets.

Third, it has to "clear the neighborhood around its orbit." This means that its orbit cannot cross over the orbit of another planet. *Uh-oh!* Pluto failed this test! Its path crosses over Neptune's.

Sorry, Pluto! But since dwarf planets have to pass only the first two tests, Pluto was named a dwarf planet. Then in 2008, *that* name was changed. Now Pluto and Eris are called "plutoids."

A lot of people are unhappy that Pluto was demoted. But Pluto fans shouldn't be too upset. Nothing has really changed. All they need is a good telescope and a clear night. Then, they'll be able to spot Pluto, far off in the solar system. It's right where it's always been.

Pluto Gets Demoted

Comprehension Check

1. Based on this passage, what do you think the word *demoted* means?

_____

Write your own sentence using the word.

_____

2. How many planets are in our solar system today?

_____

3. The word *orbit* means
   Ⓐ to travel in a circular path around something else.
   Ⓑ to be near the sun.
   Ⓒ to travel for 248 days.
   Ⓓ to be an object in motion.

4. When was the dwarf planet Eris discovered?

_____

5. Why did the astronomers decide that Pluto was no longer a planet?
   Ⓐ It was too small to be considered a planet.
   Ⓑ It fell from the sky.
   Ⓒ It didn't pass all three tests.
   Ⓓ Its orbit takes 248 years.

Pluto Gets Demoted

Planet Status: **REJECT**

For years, our solar system had nine known planets. Today, however, there are only eight. So what happened? Did one of them fall from the sky? Actually, Pluto got demoted!

Pluto, of course, is still out there where it's always been. Pluto hasn't changed, but our definition of *planets* has.

In August 2006, a group of astronomers decided that we should no longer consider Pluto a planet. They said Pluto didn't meet certain standards. Instead, they concluded, it was really a "dwarf planet."

These astronomers decided that before an object in space can be called a planet, it has to pass three basic tests:

First, it has to orbit around the sun. *Check*! Pluto travels around the sun once every 248 years. Its orbit is less circular than the other planets', but the astronomers still gave Pluto a passing grade.

Second, it has to be big enough to form a round or nearly round shape. *Check*! Like the other planets in our solar system, Pluto passes that test.

Third, it has to "clear the neighborhood around its orbit." This means that the path it travels cannot cross over the path of another planet. This last test is the one Pluto failed. Its path crosses over Neptune's.

Sorry, Pluto!

Pluto's problems started in 2005. That's when the dwarf planet Eris was discovered, out beyond Pluto. Eris is bigger than Pluto. So many astronomers wondered if Eris wasn't a planet, how could Pluto be?

In 2006, the group of astronomers made their decision. Pluto wasn't a planet after all, but was a dwarf planet, like Eris. Dwarf planets have to pass only the first two tests. In 2008 the astronomers decided to rename the dwarf planets "plutoids."

Lots of people are still angry about Pluto's demotion, even some astronomers. But Pluto fans shouldn't be too upset. All they need is a high-powered telescope and a clear night. Then, if they're lucky, they'll get a glimpse of Pluto, far off in our solar system, just where it's always been.

Pluto Gets Demoted

Comprehension Check

1. A group of astronomers decided that Pluto should no longer be considered a planet because
   Ⓐ It's really a dwarf planet.
   Ⓑ It didn't meet certain standards.
   Ⓒ There were too many planets in our solar system already.
   Ⓓ Pluto was no longer in our solar system.

2. According to the passage, Pluto hasn't changed. What has?
   Ⓐ Pluto's orbit around the sun
   Ⓑ our definition of what a planet is
   Ⓒ the name for dwarf planets
   Ⓓ Pluto's distance from Eris

3. Name one way Pluto is like the eight planets in our solar system.

   _____

   _____

4. What is the new name for a "dwarf planet"?

   _____

5. Summarize the main idea of the last paragraph.

   _____

   _____

Pluto Gets Demoted

Planet Status:
REJECT

Not very long ago, our solar system contained nine known planets. Today there are only eight. So what happened? Did one of them fall from the sky? Actually, Pluto got demoted!

Don't worry—Pluto is still out there where it's always been. It isn't Pluto that's changed, but simply our classification of it. In August 2006, an international group of astronomers decided that Pluto should no longer be considered a planet because it didn't meet certain **criteria**, or standards. Instead they reclassified it as a "dwarf planet."

In order to qualify as a planet, these astronomers decided that a celestial body has to pass three basic tests:

First, it has to orbit the sun. *Check*! Pluto completes its orbit around the sun once every 248 years. Its orbit is more elliptical than circular, but that didn't bother the astronomers.

Second, it has to be big enough to form a round or nearly round shape. *Check*! Pluto is quite a bit smaller than Mercury, the next smallest planet, but it is massive enough for its own gravity to create a spherical shape.

Third, it has to "clear the neighborhood around its orbit." This means that the path of its orbit cannot intersect with the orbit of another planet. And this last criterion is where Pluto's "planethood" bit the dust. Its orbit crosses paths with Neptune's.

Sorry, Pluto!

Pluto was discovered and declared a planet in 1930. Yet by the 1970s, astronomers had already begun to question whether it truly deserved planet status because it was so much smaller than the other planets in our solar system. Trouble for Pluto really began brewing, however, in 2005 when the dwarf planet Eris was discovered out beyond Pluto. Eris is bigger than Pluto, so if Eris wasn't a full-fledged planet, people wondered how on earth Pluto could be.

In 2006, the group of astronomers decided to strip Pluto of its full-planet status. Dwarf planets, like Eris, have to pass only the first two criteria. In 2008, a newer term, "plutoid," was proposed for these almost-planets, although not everyone is happy with that name.

Lots of people remain upset about Pluto's demotion—even some astronomers. But Pluto fans shouldn't despair. All they need is a high-powered telescope and a clear night. Then, if they're lucky, they'll get a glimpse of Pluto following its orbit, just as it's always done.

Pluto Gets Demoted

Comprehension Check

1. Explain why Pluto was demoted.

_____

_____

2. Pluto itself hasn't changed. What has?

_____

_____

3. In the fourth paragraph, the word *elliptical* is used to describe Pluto's orbit. What do you think *elliptical* means?

_____

4. The phrase "clear the neighborhood around its orbit" in the sixth paragraph is an example of

Ⓐ an opinion.

Ⓑ figurative language.

Ⓒ exaggeration.

Ⓓ foreshadowing.

5. What can you infer from this passage?

Ⓐ Several other planets in our solar system might also be demoted.

Ⓑ The astronomers thought Eris should be a planet, too.

Ⓒ Our understanding of the universe changes over time.

Ⓓ Astronomers have a hard time making up their minds.

Around the World in a Bright Pink Boat

Australian Jessica Watson is not your average teenager. At age 16, she sailed around the world. And she made the trip all by herself. She's the youngest person ever to sail the world solo.

She began her voyage in October 2009. She sailed out of Sydney Harbor in her bright pink boat. She completed the trip on May 15, 2010. She was at sea for 210 days.

Jessica had lots of sailing experience. She has been sailing since the age of eight. Even so, some people opposed the trip. They thought she was just too young. Naturally, her parents worried about her. But they trusted her skills. They believed she could safely make the trip. She was in radio contact, in case anything went wrong.

Jessica said she made the trip to challenge herself. She said she wanted to achieve something to be proud of.

People have called Jessica a hero. "I don't consider myself a hero," she said. "I'm just an ordinary girl who believed in a dream." She added, "You've got to have a dream, believe in it, and work hard."

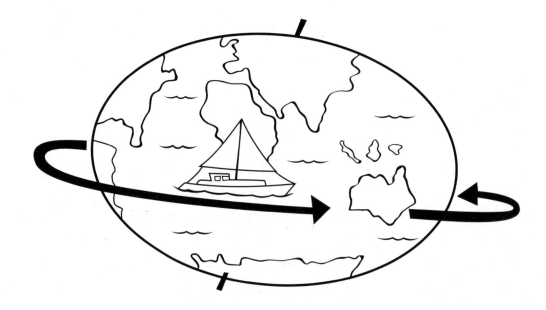

Around the World in a Bright Pink Boat

Comprehension Check

1. How old was Jessica when she sailed around the world?

_____

2. What does the word *solo* mean in paragraph 1?

   Ⓐ as a teenager

   Ⓑ alone

   Ⓒ quickly

   Ⓓ in a boat

3. How long did Jessica's trip take?

_____

4. Why did Jessica make the trip?

   Ⓐ All her friends had already done it.

   Ⓑ She wanted to improve her sailing skills.

   Ⓒ She wanted to do something she'd be proud of.

   Ⓓ Her friends dared her to do it.

5. People have called Jessica a hero. Does she agree?

_____

Around the World in a Bright Pink Boat

An Australian teen named Jessica Watson pulled off an amazing feat. At just 16, she sailed around the world. And she did it by herself! She completed her voyage on May 15, 2010. Now she's the youngest person ever to sail around the world solo.

Jessica began her trip in Sydney, Australia. She sailed in a pink yacht named *Ella's Pink Lady*. She was at sea for 210 days. When she completed her voyage, nearly 50,000 people turned up at Sydney Harbor to welcome her home.

Even though she was young, Jessica was an experienced sailor. She's been sailing since the age of eight. Still, sailing around the world alone was a daring undertaking. Some people criticized the trip, but her parents gave their approval. Of course they worried about her. But they knew she was skilled. They felt sure she could safely make the trip.

Jessica said was inspired by others who had made the trip before her. She decided to do it because she wanted to challenge herself. She said she wanted to achieve something to be proud of. And now she surely has.

Australia's Prime Minister called Jessica "Australia's newest hero." Jessica was flattered but said she disagreed. "I don't consider myself a hero," she said. "I'm an ordinary girl who believed in a dream. You've just got to have a dream, believe in it, and work hard."

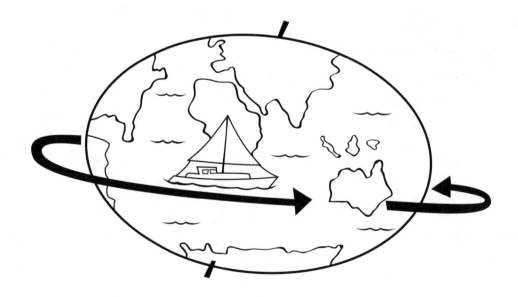

Around the World in a Bright Pink Boat

Comprehension Check

1. What does the word *solo* mean in paragraph 1?

   _____

2. Where did Jessica complete her voyage?

   _____

3. A yacht is a kind of
   - (A) sailing technique
   - (B) sailboat
   - (C) compass
   - (D) life jacket

4. What is one reason Jessica wanted to make the trip?

   _____

   _____

5. Who called Jessica a hero?

   _____

Around the World in a Bright Pink Boat

At age 16, Australian Jessica Watson did something most people twice her age would never even dream of doing. She sailed around the world nonstop. . . all by herself! When she completed her voyage on May 15, 2010, she became the youngest person ever to circumnavigate the globe alone.

Sailing on a bright pink yacht named *Ella's Pink Lady*, Jessica set out from Sydney, Australia, in October of 2009 and returned seven months later. Nearly 50,000 people turned up at Sydney Harbor to welcome her home after 210 days at sea.

Jessica has been sailing ever since the age of eight. So even before making this trip she'd logged a lot of hours on the water. She said she was inspired by others who had made the voyage before her. She decided to do the trip herself because she wanted to challenge herself and achieve something to be proud of.

Naturally, her parents worried about their daughter. But they believed she was skilled enough to make the trip safely. Some Australians publicly criticized the voyage, saying she was too young and lacked the proper experience. But in the end, she proved them wrong. Jessica safely sailed 23,000 nautical miles, encountering raucous storms, and a few waves so big they tipped her boat onto its side. She's shown the world she's a true sailor.

Upon her return, Australia's Prime Minister, Kevin Rudd, called her "Australia's newest hero." Jessica, however, disagreed. She said, "I don't consider myself a hero. I'm an ordinary girl who believed in a dream. You don't have to be someone special or anything special to achieve something amazing. You've just got to have a dream, believe in it, and work hard."

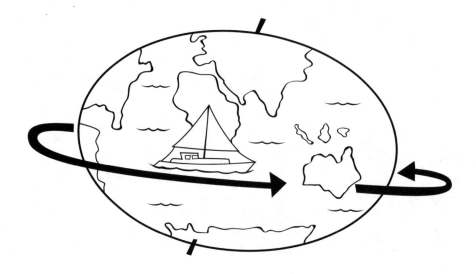

Around the World in a Bright Pink Boat

Comprehension Check

1. In the first paragraph, the word *circumnavigate* contains the prefix *circum-* and the word *navigate*. What do you think *circumnavigate* means?

_____

2. Why did so many people come out to see Jessica on her return?

_____

_____

_____

3. Why did Jessica's parents let her go on the trip?

_____

_____

4. A synonym for *raucous* in paragraph 4 is
  Ⓐ tall
  Ⓑ harsh
  Ⓒ large
  Ⓓ scary

5. Does Jessica consider herself a hero? Why or why not?

_____

_____

_____

Answer Key

The Coolest Jobs Ever?

Page 7
1. D
2. A
3. C
4. Yes. He says he has the best job in the world.
5. A   .

Page 9
1. A
2. C
3. Answer should be one of the following: travels to hotels and resorts all over the world; checks the safety of the slides; makes sure the height and speed are just right; makes sure the slides have enough water.
4. making sure new video games work the way they're supposed to
5. B

Page 11
1. Yes. She says it's one of the many cool careers out there.
2. They spend their days tasting ice cream.
3. B
4. something you like
5. D

Busy Bees

Page 13
1. A
2. C
3. B
4. about five
5. B

Page 15
1. spring and summer
2. A
3. colony
4. C
5. Answers will vary but should include evidence from the passage that the author likes bees.

Page 17
1. because bees make honey
2. females
3. B
4. A
5. Answer should include the idea that bees' hard work helps bring us food.

Bobbie the Wonder Dog

Page 19
1. C
2. C
3. B
4. D
5. Answers will vary.

Page 21
1. A
2. D
3. Answer should include the idea that it seemed unbelievable that Bobbie could have traveled all that way.
4. C
5. Answers will vary.

Page 23
1. B
2. because Bobbie was lost
3. A
4. Answers will vary.
5. Even though Bobby was a celebrity, he was happiest to be back home.

Catching Zzzz's

Page 25
1. nine to ten hours each night
2. A
3. C
4. D
5. B

Page 27
1. Sleeping
2. No, because ants and bats sleep more than giraffes.
3. B
4. D
5. C

Page 29
1. sleeping
2. B
3. Answer should be one of the following: When we sleep, we give our bodies a chance to recover from all the work we did during the day. During sleep our brains have a chance to rest and regenerate themselves.
4. B
5. B

Nightlights That Fly!

Page 31
1. lightning bugs
2. D
3. B
4. A
5. a bitter chemical that tastes really bad

Page 33
1. nocturnal
2. B
3. It's their way of talking to each other and finding a mate.
4. It helps keep predators away.
5. We get to enjoy the fireflies' glow.

Page 35
1. Possible answers: seen, spotted, spy (spied)
2. They glow.
3. Its own particular pattern of flashes, or "language"
4. B
5. Answer should give evidence from that passage that the author likes fireflies.

"Dear Aunt Edna . . ."

Page 37
1. They're all fast.
2. C
3. A
4. C
5. in trucks and airplanes

Page 39
1. Today's instant communication was introduced.
2. B
3. D
4. A
5. Because it's slower than the new, instant forms of communication we now have.

Page 41
1. the ancient Egyptians
2. A
3. C
4. the 1990s
5. They're much faster.

Practice, Practice, Practice ... Makes Perfect!
Page 43
1. A
2. about ten thousand hours
3. about ten or twelve years
4. A
5. B

Page 45
1. C
2. B
3. A
4. ten thousand hours
5. B

Page 47
1. A
2. practice a lot
3. They are examples of people who are great at what they do.
4. D
5. Answers will vary.

Lonesome George: The Last of His Kind
Page 49
1. A
2. a Pinta Island tortoise
3. C
4. 150 years
5. A

Page 51
1. B
2. He's the last living tortoise of his kind.
3. B
4. A
5. If he does, the Pinta Island tortoises won't die out.

Page 53
1. Because he's the last living Pinta Island tortoise in the world.
2. Possible answers: dead; lost; vanished
3. a smaller group within a species
4. They were killed by hunters.
5. George is responsible for their future. If George has babies, his subspecies will live on, and if he doesn't they won't.

Gimme a Slice!
Page 55
1. B
2. Naples, Italy
3. A
4. C
5. D

Page 57
1. modern pizza
2. It was cheap, and they could buy only as much as they could afford.
3. B
4. D
5. C

Page 59
1. A
2. They thought they were poisonous.
3. They weren't poisonous after all.
4. American soldiers returning from Italy wanted pizza, and the word spread.
5. B

What's the Point of Acupuncture?
Page 61
1. A
2. B
3. A
4. B
5. A

Page 63
1. stick needles in your body to make you feel better
2. thousands of years
3. B
4. The body gets sick or feels pain.
5. A

Page 65
1. To unblock the *chi* so it can flow freely, and make pain or illness go away.
2. The journalist James Reston wrote about it in *The New York Times*.
3. Possible answers: headaches, muscle strain, allergies, acne
4. A
5. Possible answer: to give a vivid picture of how thin the needles are.

Pluto Gets Demoted
Page 67
1. Answers will vary.
2. Eight
3. A
4. 2005
5. C

Page 69
1. B
2. B
3. Answer should include one of the following: It orbits around the sun. It's big enough to form a round or nearly round shape.
4. plutoid
5. Answers will vary.

Page 71
1. Answers will vary.
2. Our classification has changed; it's no longer considered a planet.
3. oval
4. B
5. C

Around the World in a Bright Pink Boat
Page 73
1. sixteen
2. B
3. 210 days
4. C
5. No

Page 75
1. alone
2. Sydney Harbor
3. B
4. The answer should include either of the following: She wanted to challenge herself. She wanted to achieve something to be proud of.
5. Australia's prime minister

Page 77
1. to travel around
2. Answers will vary.
3. They believed she was skilled enough to make the trip safely.
4. B
5. No. She says she's just an ordinary girl who worked hard to realize her dream.

References

Aamodt, S., & Wang, S. (2008). *Welcome to Your Brain*. New York: Bloomsbury USA.

Bennett, J. (2010, May 16). "Solo Sailor Jessica Watson, 16, Completes Globe-Circling Feat." *Los Angeles Times*. Retrieved from http://articles.latimes.com/2010/may/16/world/la-fg-australia-sailor-20100516

Cain, F. (2008, April 10). Why Pluto Is No Longer a Planet. Retrieved from http://www.universetoday.com/13573/why-pluto-is-no-longer-a-planet/

Gladwell, M. (2008). *Outliers: The Story of Success*. Boston: Little, Brown.

Helstosky, C. Pizza: *A Global History*. London: Reaktion Books.

Neuroscience for Kids: How Much Do Animals Sleep? (n. d.). Retrieved from http://faculty.washington.edu/chudler/chasleep.html

"Pluto-like objects now called Plutoids." (2008, June 11). *Astronomy.* Retrieved from http://www.astronomy.com/en/sitecore/content/Home/News-Observing/News/2008/06/Pluto-like%20objects%20now%20called%20Plutoids.aspx

Sleep Education Blog. (2009, July 20). Retrieved from http://sleepeducation.blogspot.com/2009/07/do-all-animals-sleep.html

Stelljes, S. (n.d.). "Bobbie the Wonder Dog." *The Oregon Encyclopedia*. Retrieved from http://www.oregonencyclopedia.org/entry/view/bobbie_the_wonder_dog/

"What Makes a Firefly Glow?" (n. d.). Retrieved from http://learn.genetics.utah.edu/content/begin/dna/firefly/

"World's Coolest Jobs." (2010, January 19). *Daily News*. Retrieved from http://www.nydailynews.com/money/galleries/worlds_coolest_jobs/worlds_coolest_jobs.html

"Why Do We Sleep, Anyway?" (2007, December 18). Retrieved from http://healthysleep.med.harvard.edu/healthy/matters/benefits-of-sleep/why-do-we-sleep